THE SUNRISE
MOVEMENT

THE SUNRISE MOVEMENT

The Climate Revolution Generation

HEATHER E. SCHWARTZ

LERNER PUBLICATIONS ◆ MINNEAPOLIS

Lerner Publications Company
An imprint of Lerner Publishing Group, Inc.
241 First Avenue North
Minneapolis, MN 55401 USA

For reading levels and more information, look up this title at www.lernerbooks.com.

Main body text set in Rotis Serif Std 55 Regular. Typeface provided by Adobe Systems.

Designer: Lauren Cooper
Lerner team: Sue Marquis

Library of Congress Cataloging-in-Publication Data

Names: Schwartz, Heather E., author.
Title: The Sunrise Movement : the climate revolution generation / Heather E. Schwartz.
Description: Minneapolis : Lerner Publications , [2023] | Series: Gateway biographies | Includes
   bibliographical references and index. | Audience: Ages 9–14 | Audience: Grades 4–6 |
   Summary: "The Sunrise Movement is a youth-led group combating climate change. Eight
   activists of various backgrounds came together and created the Sunrise Movement. Discover
   the group's goals for a greener future, their successes, and much more"– Provided by
   publisher.
Identifiers: LCCN 2022019736 (print) | LCCN 2022019737 (ebook) | ISBN 9781728476568
   (library binding) | ISBN 9781728486321 (paperback) | ISBN 9781728482705 (ebook)
Subjects: LCSH: Sunrise Movement (Organization) –Juvenile literature. | Climatic changes–
   Political aspects–United States–Juvenile literature. | Youth movements–United States–
   Juvenile literature. | Green movement–United States–Juvenile literature.
Classification: LCC QC902.8 .S45 2023 (print) | LCC QC902.8 (ebook) | DDC 320.58–dc23/
   eng20220722

LC record available at https://lccn.loc.gov/2022019736
LC ebook record available at https://lccn.loc.gov/2022019737

Manufactured in the United States of America
1-52237-50677-8/5/2022

TABLE OF CONTENTS

A Sunrise on Climate Change 9

Fighting Fossil Fuels 13

The Green New Deal 17

Launching the Sunrise Movement 22

Political Protests 25

Taking Action 28

Activism during the Pandemic 32

Vision for the Future 36

Important Dates 40
Source Notes 42
Selected Bibliography 44
Learn More 46
Index 47

Members of the Sunrise Movement advocate for climate
change legislation on December 10, 2018.

On December 10, 2018, young people lined a hallway in the Cannon House Office Building in Washington, DC, near House Representative Nancy Pelosi's office. Some held signs that read Do Your Job, Green Jobs for All, and What Is Your Plan?

The protesters cared about halting climate change. But that day, they had one goal. They needed more House Democrats to create a committee that would make climate change a priority. The issue crossed the political divide, but Democrats were more likely to support their cause.

"We are now fighting for existence," one protester said in an impassioned speech to the crowd. "This is not about Republican. This is not about Democrat. This is about humanity!"

Sunrise Movement activists gather in Nancy Pelosi's office to pressure her and other lawmakers to act on climate change in 2018.

The protesters were part of a larger movement—the Sunrise Movement, a grassroots youth-led organization determined to stop the climate crisis and build a fairer future for all. Their first sit-in at Pelosi's office a month earlier had made a real impact. About twenty-four House Democrats had been persuaded to their side. But they needed more support.

They called for a response from the leaders they were trying to reach with their message. They sang and clapped as security officers spoke into bullhorns, warning them that they would be arrested for demonstrating illegally if they didn't leave.

But the protesters had no plans to leave until their demands were heard—and met.

Media swarmed among them as they continued purposely disrupting business as usual at the Capitol. The world was getting a glimpse of the power of the Sunrise Movement. Sunrise cofounder Varshini Prakash showed up with a clear message for America's leaders. She didn't hold back.

"Today we are here to say to Democratic politicians in general that the time is enough, no more excuses," she said. "We need them to take action at the actual scale and scope of the crisis at hand."

A Sunrise on Climate Change

The Sunrise Movement is a youth movement focused on stopping climate change and creating millions of good-paying jobs. It was founded in 2017 by Sara Blazevic, Michael Dorsey, Victoria Fernandez, Dyanna Jaye, Matthew Lichtash, Stephen O'Hanlon, Varshini Prakash, and Evan Weber. They named the movement Sunrise because they wanted to work to end what they called a dark period for the US.

The founders weren't all friends before they started organizing. Most of them didn't know one another. And their backgrounds varied widely.

At eleven years old, Varshini Prakash saw a huge tsunami hit the Indian Ocean while she was watching

Varshini Prakash speaks during a 2019 climate change protest.

TV. Enormous waves killed hundreds of thousands of people in the same area of the world where her parents had emigrated from and where her grandmother still lived. Suddenly, she had a personal connection to the climate crisis.

Varshini felt powerless miles away at her home in Acton, Massachusetts. Desperate to help, she gathered canned foods and brought them to a donation box. But deep down, she knew it wasn't enough.

As she got older, that feeling of powerlessness stuck with her. She wanted to make change, but how? She didn't feel as though the leaders with real power wanted to hear from her. "Growing up as a brown, skinny, short girl, I felt that the whole culture of politics and elections and the government reveled in my exclusion," she said.

But she would later learn how much power she had.

Sara Blazevic grew up in New York City and had roots in Croatia. On visits there, she played on the banks of the Dobra River near where her family lived. When she was in college in the US, a huge storm slammed Croatia and caused massive flooding. She realized the same thing could happen in her own family's Croatian village, and climate change was to blame.

When few reporters covered the story, she worried that her family's history could be swept away, and no one would know or care.

"I realized that nobody outside of Croatia was going to fight for my family or for that place," she said. "It lit a fire under me to do that, to take seriously the power that I hold as a young person in the United States, and to do everything I can to fight to protect the people and the places that I love and care about."

Dyanna Jaye grew up by the ocean in Hampton Roads, Virginia. She watched as global warming affected her community. Because climate change was causing icebergs to melt and the sea level to rise, flooding was destroying local beaches. She saw them disappear.

She also saw what happened when her community tried to repair the damage. Hampton Roads rebuilt beaches in tourist spots and areas where wealthy people lived. But Dyanna noticed that the city didn't rebuild beaches in neighborhoods with people of color and people with low incomes. She thought this was unfair and wanted to do something about it.

"It was always about protecting the place that I love and believing that no one should have to live in fear of losing the place that they come from and call home," Jaye said.

Evan Weber grew up in O'ahu, Hawaii, and also watched his favorite beaches disappear over time. He calls it "slow violence." By the time he was an adult, many of his favorite beaches had eroded completely.

A beach eroding in O'ahu, Hawaii

One day, while walking with his mother, they reached a spot on a beach where the sand dropped off like a cliff. It was falling away into the ocean. At that moment, Weber knew exactly why he needed to work to stop climate change.

A common bond among the Sunrise Movement founders was a sense of growing up in a climate apocalypse. Their experiences told them catastrophe was a real threat. Climate change could destroy the world—unless they took action to stop it.

Fighting Fossil Fuels

When Prakash went to college at the University of Massachusetts Amherst, her life changed. She took classes, like environmental science, that helped her learn more about the world. She made new friends. One day, one of them asked her to join a demonstration. Students were planning a protest against the use of fossil fuels in infrastructure in western Massachusetts.

Prakash's friend wanted her to be the event's emcee. Prakash was terrified to stand up in front of that many people, but she agreed to do it. The closer the day came, the more stressed out and nervous she felt.

On the day of the protest, she held a megaphone in front of about one hundred other students. She talked about environmental justice, and suddenly, she wasn't scared at all. "I almost burst into tears, because standing there, for the first time in my life, I finally felt like I wasn't just this small person facing the climate crisis alone," she said. "I was powerful. I had people with me."

Prakash continued to speak up after the protest. The University of Massachusetts Amherst invested in fossil fuel companies, and she knew that was harming the environment. She helped start a campaign focused on convincing the university to stop investing in these companies.

Stephen O'Hanlon used to believe climate change wasn't real. After learning the science behind it in high school, he realized he was wrong. As a college student at Swarthmore College, he took a trip to West Virginia. He knew fossil fuels impacted the planet, but he didn't know how they affected people. On his trip he met with young people who had respiratory illnesses and cancers because they lived in coal mining communities. Mining creates dust that is harmful when inhaled.

"This was one of the poorest places in America," he said. "That made me see the issues around climate and environment in a totally different way, and made it clear this is a social justice issue."

O'Hanlon returned from the trip and started working on Swarthmore's fossil fuel divestment campaign, along with Blazevic, another student at Swarthmore. He wanted the college to stop investing in fossil fuels for the good of the environment and for the benefit of people in West Virginia and all over the world.

At the University of Virginia, Jaye started off as a

A coal mine in West Virginia

civil engineering major, but soon realized that wasn't the path she wanted to take. She wasn't sure where it would take her, but she wanted to learn more about the environment. She switched her major to environmental science and global development.

Over the next four years, she led a fossil fuel divestment effort at her school. She cofounded the Virginia Student Environmental Coalition, a statewide organization focused on climate change. And in her last year of school, she applied to be a United Nations youth delegate at the 2014 United Nations Climate Change Conference. She was selected and excited to get more involved in making a difference.

College students protest their schools' investments in fossil fuel companies in 2019.

The Green New Deal

In June 2013, President Barack Obama gave a speech at Georgetown University. He announced his Climate Action Plan. It would decrease carbon pollution, prepare the US for the results of climate change, and lead the world's efforts to address climate change. But was it enough?

Weber and Lichtash, both students at Wesleyan University, didn't think so. Neither did Michael Dorsey, an activist and visiting scholar at Wesleyan's College of the Environment. They wanted to cut emissions by more than double what the president's plan outlined. They wanted a greenhouse gas fee to motivate companies to stop using

Obama details his Climate Action Plan at Georgetown in 2013.

fossil fuels. The money collected could be used to study better energy sources and protect communities in need.

Weber, Lichtash, and Dorsey secured a $30,000 grant from Wesleyan University's Green Fund so they could spend the summer creating a better plan.

"We started coming up with an idea. What would it look like to actually demand action at the scale that was needed and put forward solutions actually at the scale of the problem?" Weber said.

The Sierra Club, a national environmental organization, gave them space to work. Over two months,

Ramón Cruz, the president of the Sierra Club, speaks at a 2021 protest. The Sierra Club helped the Sunrise Movement get its start.

they wrote "The Plan: How The U.S. Can Help Stabilize the Climate and Create a Clean Energy Future." The thirty-five-page proposal included ideas for phasing out fossil fuel use on federal land, creating a panel focused on the climate crisis, and taxing carbon use. It was a rough outline of a Green New Deal that could push for change at the highest levels of government.

While their plan was new, the idea of a Green New Deal was not. It drew from other past plans that had focused on major reform efforts, the environment, and the economy. Weber, Lichtash, and Dorsey wanted to halt the climate crisis and change the way money was spent to create a safer, more sustainable, and more just world.

FDR'S NEW DEAL

Between 1933 and 1939, President Franklin Delano Roosevelt's New Deal included a series of programs to help the US recover from the Great Depression that begin in 1929. The programs focused on helping lower-income people, stimulating the economy, and reforming financial systems that had failed.

The large-scale response to overwhelming challenges worked. FDR's New Deal was successful on many levels, and there hasn't been another Great Depression since.

The idea of a Green New Deal that can rescue the world from the ravages of climate change builds on the New Deal. With the same style of bold action and reform, activists hope a Green New Deal can have a similar positive impact.

They needed to spread the word about their ideas, so Lichtash wrote an article for *U.S. News & World Report* about their goals. He explained how investing in public transportation could help stop climate change if more people used it and if the energy sources were clean. He called Obama's plan "a step in the right direction" that they needed to build on.

"True climate leadership can only occur with the support of Congress. It is clear that politics is all that stands in our way—the technologies and policies exist to ensure a better future," he wrote.

Lichtash and Weber continued their activism in other ways too. Lichtash started working for the New York Power Authority and used his position to push for the use of electric vehicles. Weber waited tables and did bike deliveries, but he also networked with other activists and traveled to attend protests. In 2014 he went to the People's

WHAT IS CLIMATE CHANGE?

Climate change causes warmer weather. But the critical issues created by climate change include dangerous storms and other problems for the planet, such as droughts, heat waves, and wildfires. Scientists have evidence that human use of fossil fuels is largely to blame.

Over 300,000 people attended the 2014 People's Climate March in New York City.

Climate March in New York City, where he met Jaye. The future founders of the Sunrise Movement were finding one another. They shared a passion for the same cause and their common goals drew them together.

Launching the Sunrise Movement

In 2016 Blazevic, Dorsey, Fernandez, Jaye, Lichtash, O'Hanlon, Prakash, and Weber wanted former Secretary of State Hillary Clinton to win the US presidential election. They thought she'd listen to their proposals to fight climate change and would pass legislation to do so. But Donald Trump was elected. He did not believe in global warming. He planned to end Obama's policies that protected the environment.

When Trump became president, the activists were alarmed. The election was on their minds as they worked to make the Sunrise Movement official. It took nine months to carefully plan the launch. In April 2017, the eight founders created the Sunrise Movement as a nonprofit, with the plan to focus on both protests and elections.

The Sierra Club and 350.org gave the Sunrise activists money to form their movement. Both international organizations want to end the use of fossil fuels and replace it with renewable energy. But they still weren't well known. Some movements become well known quickly but also disappear quickly. It was important to the Sunrise Movement that they would be able to last so they could build a greener future.

By November 2018, Sunrise had eleven small hubs, or local centers, where activists worked across the country. They held meetings, attended rallies, made phone calls, participated in social media projects, and more. That month Sunrise took action in a big way, calling major attention to their efforts.

350.org activists demonstrate the dangers of rising waters in 2010.

SUNRISE'S NONPROFIT STATUS

Nonprofit organizations like the Sunrise Movement are allowed to operate without paying taxes to the government because they are working for the public's benefit. This saves the organization money. But funds are still needed to keep a nonprofit running.

Nonprofits have many of the same costs as other organizations, which may include salaries for employees, rent, and bills for heating and electricity. Sunrise had about sixteen full-time staff members by the end of 2018. The organization rents workspace from the Sierra Club in Washington, DC.

WHO IS RESPONSIBLE?

Individuals can reduce the use of fossil fuels by driving less, using public transportation, buying energy efficient appliances, and consuming fewer goods. But the biggest culprits are large corporations. In 2017 one hundred companies were identified as responsible for more than 70 percent of greenhouse gas emissions causing climate change.

A power plant that burns fossil fuels to create electricity

Political Protests

The activists in the Sunrise Movement expected Democratic leaders to take up their cause and support measures that would halt climate change. But they wanted to make sure a plan was in place while Trump was in office. His agenda was moving in the opposite direction. Throughout 2018, his administration proposed cuts to spending on clean energy programs, started undoing Obama's new standards to make cars and trucks more energy efficient, and created a plan that would weaken rules curbing coal mine pollution.

Sunrise activists couldn't stop what was happening, but they wanted to be prepared for the future. They looked forward to when Democratic leaders would have more power and could take action.

In November, Pelosi announced plans for a committee to address the issues that mattered to Sunrise. But she also said the committee would not have real power. It would not be set up to change laws and make lasting change. To Sunrise, this was not nearly enough. They wanted a committee to draft legislation, and they were ready to fight for it.

On November 13, about two hundred Sunrise activists staged a protest at Pelosi's office. Most of the activists that day were teenagers and in their early twenties, proving that the Sunrise Movement was powered by a strong base of committed youth.

"Almost everybody in Sunrise has lived our entire lives in a world on the cusp of climate apocalypse,"

Blazevic said. "That's what drives them—just the sheer scale of the devastation on the horizon."

For hours, the protesters sang songs and shouted their demands, purposefully creating a disruptive atmosphere. They refused to leave, and about fifty were arrested. But the movement got a boost when Representative Alexandria Ocasio-Cortez joined them to show her support. She high-fived protesters. Protesters clapped and cheered.

"I just want to let you all know how proud I am of each and every single one of you for putting yourselves and your bodies and everything on the line to make sure that we save our planet, our generation, and our future," she said. "It's so incredibly important."

Later that day, Ocasio-Cortez proposed the creation of a select committee that would focus on the Green New Deal. Unlike Pelosi's proposed committee, it would have the power to draft legislation. Soon after, Pelosi announced plans to reinstate a climate change committee and allow for their climate protests to go on.

Sunrise wanted even stronger support. But clearly the movement was making a difference. Several members of Congress were convinced it was time to work toward 100 percent renewable energy in the US. They publicly said they supported the formation of Ocasio-Cortez's select committee. And the media was paying attention. That would help their cause. "The action was a breakthrough moment," Fernandez said. "Our wildest dreams came true: Thousands of people started walking into the movement."

ALEXANDRIA OCASIO-CORTEZ

In 2018 Alexandria Ocasio-Cortez made history when she was elected to the House of Representatives. At twenty-nine, she was the youngest woman elected to the House. She had a background in activism, having worked with Dreamers and other undocumented immigrants. She campaigned on progressive ideas such as housing as a human right and an end to police violence. As soon as she took office, she proved she also cared deeply about environmental justice.

Ocasio-Cortez speaks at a rally organized by the Sunrise Movement in 2021.

On December 10, 2018, members of the Sunrise Movement gathered outside of Pelosi's office. They wanted leaders of the Democratic Party to support the Green New Deal and form a select committee to address climate change. Showing up was a loud and clear message to politicians that if Democrats wanted the youth vote in 2020, they needed to work on this cause that meant so much to young people.

Once again, Sunrise activists loudly made their demands heard in Washington, DC. Over 130 protesters were arrested. But the protest won over more Democrats, who supported their cause. The Green New Deal was making progress.

Taking Action

The Sunrise Movement continued to grow, and by September 2019, activists worked to fight climate change at 290 hubs around the country. At that time, about fifteen thousand activists were coming to Sunrise protests in person, while eighty thousand were involved in other actions, such as emailing and calling representatives.

Some activists didn't just work together, they also lived together. This allowed them to focus on fighting climate change. These apartments and houses were called movement houses and were in Washington, DC, Pennsylvania, and Michigan. The homes were decorated

QUEER EYE CONNECTION

Season 5 of Netflix's reality show *Queer Eye* featured one of Sunrise's young activists. Eighteen-year-old Abby Leedy took a year off from college to work for the movement. But she was working so hard that her parents were worried. She was missing out on seeing friends and sometimes even forgot to eat. The hosts of the show, known as the Fab Five, helped her find a better balance between her work and her personal life. And by appearing on the show, Leedy also drew attention to the issue of climate justice. Viewers learned about her life in a "movement house" and her work speaking out at rallies and organizing protests.

The Fab Five (*from left to right*): Jonathan Van Ness, Bobby Berk, Tan France, Antoni Prowoski, and Karamo Brown, attend an award show in 2019.

with posters and banners about climate change. As Sunrise grew, so did its "movement houses."

People who centered their lives on the movement knew they were choosing activism over a more traditional path. Some gave up college, at least temporarily. Others put off buying their own homes, getting married, and having children.

"I would not know how to live with myself if I were not involved," twenty-one-year-old Sunrise activist Christian Galo told Vox.

By fall 2019, the Green New Deal was the focus of the Sunrise Movement's long-term plan. Activists wanted the US to be carbon neutral by 2030. During the time in between, fossil fuels were causing Earth's temperature to rise too quickly toward a dangerous high. As it rose, severe weather would only get worse. If it got too high, warm water coral reefs would die. Mosquitos and ticks would spread disease more easily. People would suffer from food shortages.

The 2030 deadline was a huge goal because it would mean everyone in the country, including businesses, would have to give up fossil fuels. The benefits of reducing the use of fossil fuels would outweigh the time and energy that would be needed to put the plans in place. Not only would the Green New Deal help halt climate change, but it would also create millions of jobs in renewable energy, such as green engineering, sustainable farming, and work in architecture, mechanics, and contracting.

Sunrise Movement activists protest to gain lawmakers' support for the Green New Deal in 2019.

The Sunrise Movement also had a five-year plan. Getting a Green New Deal was a part of it. That meant they wanted a carbon neutral US by 2030 and an economy that would support renewable energy. Knowing Democrats were more likely to support their efforts, their plan hinged on getting Democrats elected at every level in 2020. The goal was a Democratic president as well as majority in the House of Representatives and the Senate. Making that happen meant more efforts had to be made to motivate young voters.

Still, strikes and protests were an important part of the Sunrise Movement, and they continued on a large scale. On September 20, 2019, Sunrise joined the Global Climate Strike. More than eight hundred marches took place all over the US, proving Sunrise activists were far from alone in their fight for climate justice.

Activism during the Pandemic

In January 2020, the Sunrise Movement said it was critical for young people to be involved in the upcoming election. The country could either turn toward addressing climate change and inequities among people living in the US, or it could continue on a path that was irreparably damaging the planet and tearing people apart.

"This is going to be a pivotal year—not just for our generation, but for every single generation that will follow us for centuries to come," Jaye wrote on Sunrise's website. "In the next 12 months, we need to bring in as many people as possible into the movement."

LOBBYING LEGISLATORS

Oil companies that produce and use fossil fuels fight regulations. They know that new laws to reduce carbon emissions will cost them money. So, the companies spend millions of dollars on lobbying to convince legislators to allow business as usual.

THE GLOBAL CLIMATE STRIKES

When Sunrise activists took to the streets on September 20, 2019, they joined like-minded people all over the world who wanted to draw attention to the climate crisis and inspire leaders to act. Teen activist Greta Thunberg marched with students in New York City. Millions of people around the world marched. It was the largest action for climate justice in history.

Thousands of people protested for environmental justice in New York City on September 20, 2019. About four million people participated in strikes around the world.

Sunrise planned to grow their movement. They wanted to keep organizing, protesting, and motivating people to vote. But their plans would have to change. A virus was spreading, and in March, the World Health Organization had declared a pandemic. The US went into lockdown, closing schools and businesses to prevent people from gathering and spreading COVID-19.

Sunrise canceled their protests, including the one planned for the fiftieth anniversary of Earth Day in April. They had to find other ways to engage with people, and their youth was a huge advantage.

"We're an organization of a bunch of millennials and Generation Z so in many ways we grew up online and are well-equipped to meet this moment," Weber said.

The movement launched Sunrise School to teach high school and college students about organizing and campaigning through online classes. Since it looked as though Biden was going to be the Democratic presidential candidate on the ballot in November, the activists also worked with other organizations on a list of demands for him to meet if he wanted to win the youth vote. Voter turnout was a major focus for Sunrise as the year continued.

Throughout 2020, Sunrise reached out to more than 6.5 million young voters. Activists mailed more than seven hundred thousand postcards. They sent 2.6 million texts and made 5.8 million calls. It was all part of an organized effort to elect candidates who would support the Green New Deal, including Biden, who became the Democrats' presidential nominee in August.

BIDEN'S NUMBER ONE PRIORITY: CLIMATE CHANGE

In October 2020, with the presidential election just weeks away, Biden called climate change "the number one issue facing humanity." He said addressing it was his top priority. Sunrise wanted this kind of commitment from a Democratic presidential candidate. His words were a rallying cry for young voters. They turned out in droves, including in the key election states of Arizona, Georgia, Michigan, and Pennsylvania, to make sure he was elected.

They motivated the biggest youth voter turnout in history. Biden won the presidential election. Sunrise was prepared and put the pressure on immediately, urging Biden to act boldly and use the climate crisis to unite the divided country. On its website, Sunrise listed top picks for Biden in building his leadership team. Sunrise also wanted Biden to establish a new executive office—the Office of Climate Mobilization—to cut ties with fossil fuel companies and fight the climate crisis.

Biden was sworn into office on January 20, 2021. The following day was his first full day in office. Sunrise planned a day of action for that day to push for what they wanted: financial relief that would go directly to people,

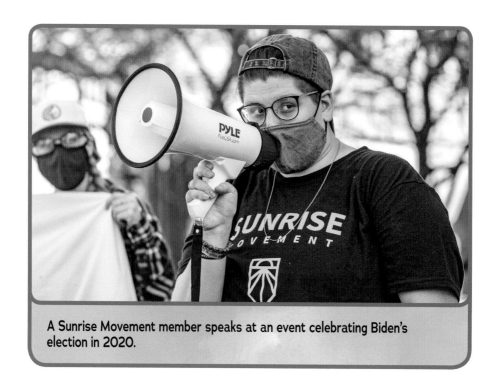

A Sunrise Movement member speaks at an event celebrating Biden's election in 2020.

a multiracial democracy, millions of good jobs, and an end to both systemic inequality and the climate crisis. Activists all over the country showed up at congressional members' offices and homes to march and rally. They created a virtual space for activists to gather and work together too. It was all part of Sunrise's mission to build a better future for all.

Vision for the Future

When Biden took office, one of his first actions was the creation of the National Climate Task Force. It would mobilize the federal government to fight climate change by curbing emissions, conserving land, and protecting public health. He also organized the Leaders Summit on Climate, a gathering of more than forty world leaders focused on addressing the climate crisis.

Sunrise celebrated these victories. The activists knew these steps were only the beginning. But it looked as though the country was starting to move in the right direction on climate change.

Though the pandemic continued, many restrictions were lifted and eased. Sunrise got back to more in-person activities throughout the year. On Earth Day in April 2021, Sunrise activists gathered at Mount Tabor, an area in Portland, Oregon, to celebrate the planet they were fighting for. They dressed up, danced to live music, and listened to speakers. Sunrise hubs held events and protests in other areas of the country.

In August, Sunrise held its first Movement Leaders x All Hands call event, a gathering focused on bringing leaders and staff together to build relationships, share updates, and celebrate wins. Sunrise was growing and organizing to be more effective. The activists carefully watched what political and corporate leaders were doing so they could plan and take action to drive decisions in a direction that would address the climate crisis.

By the end of 2021, Sunrise was in phase 5 of its long-term Green New Deal strategy. The movement was launched, they'd pushed their agenda into elections, and they'd brought attention to their cause throughout the

TROUBLE WITHIN

Sunrise has fought for racial equality and justice in its work, but in 2021, the movement was criticized as racist. Some members believed the leadership wasn't diverse enough. They felt the movement was using people of color for appearances only. Some felt underpaid and overworked too. About one hundred activists came forward.

In response, Sunrise committed to changing policies and transforming the organization for more equity. Ending the climate crisis is an ongoing fight. The same is true for ensuring the movement is fair to everyone involved.

country. The activists were looking toward the 2022 elections, trying to get people who supported the Green New Deal elected. Then it would be easier for Congress to pass the plan.

In five years, Sunrise accomplished more than anyone could have imagined. And young people were the driving force. Some of the founders had started the movement believing they didn't have a voice at all. Now leaders are listening to them. Sunrise activist saw the chance to step up and make change—and they did.

"Politics doesn't have to be this thing that is inaccessible to all of us. It is what we make of it when

Sunrise Movement members march in 2021 to gain support for climate change legislation.

we participate," Prakash said. "A lot of ordinary kids who have a vision, a dream, a drive, and a passion and compassion for the world around them, is the ultimately motivating force that can change the world."

IMPORTANT DATES

2013   President Barack Obama announces his Climate Action Plan.

Weber, Dorsey, and Lichtash write "The Plan: How the U.S. Can Help Stabilize the Climate and Create a Clean Energy Future."

2014   Weber and Jaye meet at the People's Climate March in New York City.

2016   Donald Trump is elected president of the United States.

2017   The Sunrise Movement is established as a nonprofit.

2018   Alexandria Ocasio-Cortez is elected to the House of Representatives.

Sunrise activists protest at House Representative Nancy Pelosi's office.

2019	Sunrise activists join the Global Climate Strike.
2020	Sunrise contacts more than 6.5 million young voters.
	Joe Biden is elected president of the United States.
2021	The first Movement Leaders x All Hands call brings Sunrise leaders and staff together to build relationships, share updates, and celebrate wins.
	Work begins to ensure racial equity within Sunrise.
2022	Sunrise focuses on passing the Green New Deal.

SOURCE NOTES

7 "Climate Protest at Pelosi's Office Spurs Arrests," YouTube video, 2:40, posted by AP Archive, December 16, 2018, https://www.youtube.com/watch?v=MVbPSJfwfEU.

9 Miranda Green and Timothy Cama, "More Protesters Storm Pelosi's Office Demanding Climate Change Action," Hill, December 10, 2018, https://thehill.com/policy/energy-environment/420588-second-round-of-capitol-protests-demand-climate-change-action/.

11 Erza Klein, "'No Permanent Friends, No Permanent Enemies': Inside the Sunrise Movement's Plan to Save Humanity," Vox, July 31, 2019, https://www.vox.com/ezra-klein-show-podcast/2019/7/31/20732041/varshini-prakash-sunrise-movement-green-new-deal.

11 Sara Blazevic, "Sara: New York, New York," interview, Our Climate Voices, June 13, 2017, https://www.ourclimatevoices.org/2017/sara.

12 "Interview with Dyanna Jaye, Sunrise Movement, 2019 Visionary Leaders Award Recipient," Physicians for Social Responsibility, October 31, 2019, https://www.psr.org/blog/interview-with-dyanna-jaye-sunrise-movement-2019-visionary-leaders-award-recipient/.

12 "Evan, O'ahu, Hawaii," interview, Our Climate Voices, May 24, 2017, https://www.ourclimatevoices.org/2017/evan.

13–14 Klein, "'No Permanent Friends, No Permanent Enemies': Inside the Sunrise Movement's Plan to Save Humanity."

14 Nicole Javorsky, "A 23-year-old Sunrise Movement Founder Says the 'Adults in the Room' Aren't Taking Climate Change Seriously," *Mother Jones,* August 28, 2019, https://www.motherjones.com/politics/2019/08/sunrise-movement-dnc-climate-change-debate/.

18 Ella Nilsen, "The New Face of Climate Activism Is Young, Angry—and Effective," Vox, September 17, 2019, https://www.vox.com/the-highlight/2019/9/10/20847401/sunrise-movement-climate-change-activist-millennials-global-warming.

20   Michael Shank and Matt Lichtash, "Five Steps America Must Take Now to Combat Climate Change," *U.S. News & World Report*, October 15, 2013, https://www.usnews.com/opinion/blogs/world-report/2013/10/15/five-steps-america-must-take-now-to-combat-global-warming.

25–26   Chloe Malle, "Inside the Sunrise Movement: Six Weeks with the Young Activists Defining the Climate Debate," *Vogue*, September 20, 2019, https://www.vogue.com/article/inside-sunrise-movement-youth-activists-climate-debate.

26   Rex Santus, "Alexandria Ocasio-Cortez Visited Nancy Pelosi's Office—to Join a Protest," Vice News, November 13, 2018, https://www.vice.com/en/article/pa5bxz/alexandria-ocasio-cortez-visited-nancy-pelosis-office-to-join-a-protest.

26   Zahra Hirji and Ryan Brooks, "Inside "The Very Secret History" of the Sunrise Movement," BuzzFeed, August 21, 2021, https://www.buzzfeednews.com/article/zahrahirji/sunrise-movement-climate-change-black-activists.

30   Nilsen, "The New Face of Climate Activism Is Young, Angry—and Effective."

32   Dyanna Jaye, "2020 Is Here and It's All up for Grabs," Sunrise Movement, January 2, 2020, https://www.sunrisemovement.org/movement-updates/2020-is-here-and-it-s-all-up-for-grabs-6b74cbcd06d9/.

34   Zack Colman, "Climate Activists Shift Gears in an Age of 'Social Distancing,'" *Politico*, March 19, 2020, https://www.politico.com/news/2020/03/19/climate-activists-social-distancing-coronavirus-137216.

35   Emma Newburger, "Joe Biden Calls Climate Change the 'Number One Issue Facing Humanity,'" CNBC, October 24, 2020, https://www.cnbc.com/2020/10/24/joe-biden-climate-change-is-number-one-issue-facing-humanity.html.

38–39   Gary M. Kramer, "Sunrise Movement's Varshini Prakash on Not Losing Hope on Climate Change: 'I'm Still Here Fighting,'" Salon, January 23, 2022, https://www.salon.com/2022/01/23/varshini-prakash-to-the-end-build-back-better-climate-change/.

SELECTED BIBLIOGRAPHY

"Fact Sheet: Timeline of Progress Made in Obama's Climate Action Plan." Environmental and Energy Study Institute, August 5, 2015. https://www.eesi.org/papers/view/fact-sheet-timeline-progress-of-president-obama-climate-action-plan.

Green, Miranda, and Timothy Cama. "More Protesters Storm Pelosi's Office Demanding Action." Hill, December 10, 2018. https://thehill.com/policy/energy-environment/420588-second-round-of-capitol-protests-demand-climate-change-action/.

Jaye, Dyanna. "2020 Is Here and It's All up for Grabs." Sunrise Movement, January 2, 2020. https://www.sunrisemovement.org/movement-updates/2020-is-here-and-it-s-all-up-for-grabs-6b74cbcd06d9/.

Kelly, Jane. "Student Spotlight: Passion Leads Student to U.N. Conference on Climate Change." *UVA Today*, February 9, 2015. https://news.virginia.edu/content/student-spotlight-passion-leads-student-un-conference-climate-change.

Klein, Ezra. "'No Permanent Friends, No Permanent Enemies': Inside the Sunrise Movement's Plan to Save Humanity." Vox, July 31, 2019. https://www.vox.com/ezra-klein-show-podcast/2019/7/31/20732041/varshini-prakash-sunrise-movement-green-new-deal.

Kramer, Gary M. "Sunrise Movement's Varshini Prakash on Not Losing Hope on Climate Change: 'I'm Still Here Fighting.'" Salon, January 23, 2022. https://www.salon.com/2022/01/23/varshini-prakash-to-the-end-build-back-better-climate-change/.

Malle, Chloe. "Inside the Sunrise Movement: Six Weeks with the Young Activists Defining the Climate Debate." *Vogue*, September 20, 2019. https://www.vogue.com/article/inside-sunrise-movement-youth -activists-climate-debate.

Matthews, Mark K., Nick Bowlin, and Benjamin Hulac. "Inside the Sunrise Movement (It Didn't Happen by Accident)." *E&E News*, December 3, 2018. https://www.eenews.net/articles/inside-the -sunrise-movement-it-didnt-happen-by-accident/.

Rockwell, Cynthia. "Lichtash '13, Weber '13 Offer 'The Plan' to Combat Global Warming." Wesleyan Connection, November 8, 2013. https:// newsletter.blogs.wesleyan.edu/2013/11/08/globalwarming/.

Shank, Michael, and Matt Lichtash. "Five Steps America Must Take Now to Combat Climate Change." *U.S. News & World Report*, October 15, 2013. https://www.usnews.com/opinion/blogs/world-report/2013 /10/15/five-steps-america-must-take-now-to-combat-global -warming.

LEARN MORE

Harman, Alice. *Climate Change and How We'll Fix It.* New York: Union Square Kids, 2021.

Leigh, Anna. *Alexandria Ocasio-Cortez: Political Headliner.* Minneapolis: Lerner Publications, 2020.

Leonard, Jill. *Who Is Greta Thunberg?* New York: Penguin Workshop, 2020.

NASA: Climate Kids
https://climatekids.nasa.gov/climate-change-meaning/

Sierra: "Varshini Prakash on Redefining What's Possible"
https://www.sierraclub.org/sierra/2021-1-january-february/feature/varshini-prakash-redefining-whats-possible

Sunrise Movement Official Site
https://www.sunrisemovement.org

INDEX

Biden, Joe, 34–36
Blazevic, Sara, 9, 11, 14, 22, 26

Climate Action Plan, 17
Clinton, Hillary, 22
COVID-19, 34

Dorsey, Michael, 9, 17–19, 22
Dreamers, 27

Earth Day, 34, 37

Fernandez, Victoria, 9, 22, 26

Global Climate Strike, 32
Green New Deal, 19, 26, 28, 30, 34,
    37–38

Jaye, Dyanna, 9, 11–12, 14, 21–22, 32

Leaders Summit on Climate, 37
Lichtash, Matthew, 9, 17–20, 22

National Climate Task Force, 36

Ocasio-Cortez, Alexandria, 26–27
O'Hanlon, Stephen, 9, 14, 22

Pelosi, Nancy, 7–8, 25–26
People's Climate March, 20–21
Prakash, Varshini, 9–10, 13–14, 22, 39

Sierra Club, 18, 22–23
Swarthmore College, 14

350.org, 22
Thunberg, Greta, 33

Weber, Evan, 9, 12–13, 17–19, 22, 34
Wesleyan University, 17–18

PHOTO ACKNOWLEDGMENTS

Image credits: REUTERS/Evelyn Hockstein/Alamy Stock Photo, p. 2; AP Photo/Michael Brochstein/Sipa USA, pp. 6, 8, 31; AP Photo/Ron Adar/SOPA Images/Sipa USA, p. 10; Andre Seale/VW PICS/Universal Images Group/Getty Images, p. 12; Joseph Sohm/Shutterstock, p. 15; Nic Antaya/The Boston Globe/Getty Images, p. 16; AP Photo/Charles Dharapak, p. 17; Shannon Finney/Getty Images, p. 18; AP Photo/Jason DeCrow, p. 21; AP Photo/Eduardo Verdugo, p. 23; Jrs Jahangeer/Shutterstock, p. 24; Chip Somodevilla/Getty Images, p. 27; AP Photo/Richard Shotwell/Invision, p. 29; AP Photo/Michael Nigro/Sipa USA, p. 33; AP Photo/Paul Weaver/Sipa USA, p. 36; Allison Bailey/Alamy Stock Photo, p. 39.
Cover image: AP Photo/Caroline Brehman/CQ Roll Call.